ONE FOR THE ...

T0079934

One for the Rose

POEMS BY
PHILIP LEVINE

Carnegie Mellon University Press
Pittsburgh 1999

My thanks to the editors of the following publications in which these poems first appeared.

ANTAEUS ("The Conductor of Nothing")

CODY'S CALENDAR ("You Can Cry")

FIELD ("The Voice")

THE HUDSON REVIEW ("Roofs," "To a New Mother," & "The Window")

MICHIGAN QUARTERLY REVIEW ("The Doctor of Starlight")

MISSOURI REVIEW ("Depot Bay" & "I Wanted You to Know")

MOONS & LION TALES ("Making Soda Pop")

NEW ENGLAND REVIEW ("Above Jazz" & "Belief")

THE NEW YORKER ("Ascension," "The Fox," "Get Up," "I Remember Clifford," "I Was Born in Lucerne," "Never Before," "One for the Rose," "On My Own," "Rain Downriver," "Steel," "The Suit," "Sources," & "The Poem of Flight")

POETRY ("Buying Earth," "The First Truth," "Having Been Asked 'What is a Man?' I Answer," "Keep Talking," "My Name," "The Myth," "One," "The Radio," "Salt," "That Day," & "To Cipriano, in the Wind")

POETRY EAST ("Genius" & "Rain")

TWO PEARS PRESS ("Each Dawn")

My thanks to the John Simon Guggenheim Memorial Foundation for a grant which allowed me to complete this book.

My deepest thanks to my wife, my other friends, and my readers whose encouragement is here.

Library of Congress Catalog Card Number 98-71941
ISBN 0-88748-307-0

First Carnegie Mellon University Press Edition, March 1999.

One for the Rose was first published by Atheneum, New York, in 1981.

The publisher expresses gratitude to William Heyen and Thom Ward for their assistance in producing this volume.

Publication of this book is supported by gifts to the Classic Contemporaries Series from James W. Hall, Richard M. Cyert (1921-1998), and other anonymous benefactors.

This one is for Mark, John, & Teddy

CONTENTS

I

II

I

THE POEM OF FLIGHT

I shall begin with a rose for courage
and a rich green lawn where the crash occurs
with a sound like an old bridge gasping
under a load, and a white country house
from which a lady and her servants stream
toward the twisted moth. I would be
the original pilot, thirty-one, bare-headed,
my curly brown hair cut short and tinged
with blood from a wounded left hand
that must be attended to. Only an hour
before it was a usual summer morning,
warm and calm, in North Carolina,
and the two hectic brothers had laid aside
their bicycles and were busily assembling
the struts, wires, strings, and cranking
over the tiny engine. I faced the wind,
a cigarette in one hand, a map of creation
in the other. Silently I watch my hand
disappear into the white gauze the lady
turns and turns. I am the first to fly,
and the time has come to say something
to a world that largely crawls, forwards
or backwards, begging for some crust
of bread or earth, enough for a bad life
or a good death. I've returned because
thin as I am there came a moment
when not to seemed foolish and difficult
and because I've not yet tired
of the warm velvet dusks of this country
of firs and mountain oak. And because
high above the valleys and streams
of my land I saw so little of what is here,
only the barest whiff of all I eat each day.
I suppose I must square my shoulders,
lean back, and say something else,
something false, something that even I
won't understand about why some of us

3

must soar or how we've advanced beyond
the birds or that not having wings
is an illusion that a man with my money
refuses to see. It is hard to face
the truth, this truth or any other,
that climbing exhausts me, and the more
I climb, the higher I get, the less I
want to go on, and the noise is terrible,
I thought the thing would come apart,
and finally there was nothing there.

THE MYTH

She renamed me after a bridge in the hope
I would go somewhere or reach something new,
but I went on being myself, stubborn,
truculent, stupid. She combed my hair
and even put a few tired roses in among
the curls, which I threw in the garbage
the first chance I got. I would stand
on the porch and wave at the drivers
passing on their way to market while I
mumbled to myself, I hope you all starve!
No one ever said I was nice, and one
cousin even suggested I wear a collar;
that was after I climbed on the table
one Thanksgiving and stuck my nose
into the sweet potatoes and marshmallows,
which my blond son called "marsh meadows."
But my wife loved me as no one else
could, and so I was allowed to run free
crashing through the berry bushes and nettles
like a wild dog, baying at the moon
on long summer nights until the neighbors
turned up their stereos, sleeping when
and where I chose under a blanket of stars
and waking to mornings of peace among doves
who mourned the lives of doves. I never wept
because life was what it was, and when
my boys came home from college gleaming
in their pickup trucks, I sat quietly
and listened to the annals of sport
and the lies of women in their dormitories,
"townies" they called them. Having been
here all my life, a self-made man, I knew
none of this. Formed of so much sky
and stagnant water and the deepest yearnings
of the dead, I had entered this world
all at once as a myth does, believed
and generous, and like a myth, doomed

to spend eternity in the echoing halls
of libraries or gazing through the calm eyes
of stone that greet the traveller returning
from decades at sea. But for the present
in this interlude between one short life
and one long one, I bow my head each day
to the weather and love the dark truths
at the center of each human eye and sing
out of key to the ocean of joy that ebbs
and flows in my cold and secret heart.
I sing, "Don't forget me!" but I don't care
because the wind always blows, the stars
sweep onward on their fixed courses, and even
the great seas are slowly coming to bed.

TO A NEW MOTHER

for Marcia

You will come to see this son
as one child among the stars—
for that is where he really lives—
who has come down for a time
to burden your arms and disturb
the quiet of your house. Be wise
and give him not one but many names,
for though you will love him
as your own, let him be all
the children who will never bear
your name as well as this one.
When you sing him the songs
you write, turn your face away
upwards to the moonless sky
and close your eyes. Out of the chaos
of all those forgotten full moons
one face will swim forth as featureless
and cold as new silver. That is the face
of the child each of us gave the world
and the world refused.
                          Yes, you hold
two tight little fists of a boy
in tears who entered a world
that said no to all of us. Don't
tell him, don't go to the window
and cry out against anything.
Close your eyes, and he will too,
and both of you can sleep until
the sun breaks over the cold town
and the small lights catch hold
in separate houses and we waken
to a day like any other. If you wash
his hands and face and clean
the moonlight gently from his eyes,
then I'll wash my own. I'll bend
to the trough of cold, still water

and break the surface that held
my face calmly for a moment. So now
each of us three is somewhere
in the world, someone entering again
on an ordinary Wednesday in winter
with maybe a thank you, maybe a song.

GET UP

Morning wakens on time
in sub-freezing New York City.
I don't want to get out,
thinks the nested sparrow,
I don't want to get out
of my bed, says my son,
but out in Greenwich Street
the trucks are grinding and honking
at United Parcel, and the voices
of loud-speakers command us all.
The woman downstairs turns
on the TV, and the smoke
of her first sweet joint rises
toward the infinite stopping
for the duration in my nostrils.
The taxpayers of hell are voting
today on the value of garbage,
the rivers are unfreezing
so that pure white swans may ride
upstream toward the secret source
of sweet waters, all the trains
are on time for the fun of it.
It is February of the year 1979
and my 52nd winter is turning
toward spring, toward cold rain
which gives way to warm rain
and beaten down grass. If I
were serious I would say I
take my stand on the edge
of the future tense and offer
my life, but in fact I stand
before a smudged bathroom mirror
toothbrush in hand and smile
at the puffed face smiling
back out of habit. Get up,
honey, I say, it could be worse,
it could be a lot worse,
it could be happening to you.

MY NAME

A child saw my name passing into
the slow pink clouds that crawl
toward the setting sun, and he said,
"Philip Levine?" as though somehow
he should have known the name or
its meaning, and so I lived another day
but only as that sound and an exhalation
smelling of chocolate milk. That night
the letters lost each other in the dark,
and when the new day dawned there
were only the "L" and the "e" that
had held together, now circling above
Ontario in search of a masculine
French noun. Both the big and little "P"s
had gone down in the Detroit River
as, living, I had the sense never to do
and sank like broken wheels turning
and turning on no axles until they
came to rest on the silent floor
beside the jewelled and shattered
sunglasses of Morgan the Pirate. The "v"
is another story, hopeless in the telling.
The "h" was never happy doing so little.
The three "i"s, having become tired of being
even the least part of a man, went off
in search of three new legs. The little "l"
and the other "e" groped toward each other
like lovers in hell, and with the wind
blowing the heavy sulfurous air
of Delray, Michigan through their souls
they were in hell. That left only
the one "n," which had lived with me
at ease as though it were my nose
or said "notorious" to a world
that forgot I was born to make trouble.
That "n" is there now, stubborn and loyal,
eating the disgusting smoke of breweries

and drinking the exotic cordials that leak
from the thousand and one chrome shops
that were my home. All of me is crowded
into that small "n," my fears, my hopes,
my gleaming memories of rain, the tears
I never learned to surrender and the few
that fell of their own accord, the scars
on my shoulder, all my missing teeth,
the great belches I bequeathed to each dawn,
all of me huddled in one letter that says
"nothing" or "nuts" or "no one" or "never"
or "nobody gives a shit." But says it
with style the way a studious boy learns
to talk while he smokes a cigarette or pick
his nose just when the cantor soars before
him into a heaven of meaningless words.

I WAS BORN IN LUCERNE

Everyone says otherwise. They take me
to a flat on Pingree in Detroit
and say, Up there, the second floor. I say,
No, in a small Italian hotel overlooking
the lake. No doctor, no nurse. Just
a beautiful single woman who preferred
to remain that way and raise me to
the proper height, weight, and level of audacity.
They show me a slip of paper that says,
"Ford Hospital, Dr. Smear, male," and all
the rest of the clichés I could have lived by.
All that afternoon my mother held me close
to her side and watched the slow fog lift
and the water and sky blue all at once,
then darken to a deeper blue that turned
black at last, as I faced the longest night
of my life with tight fists and closed eyes
beside a woman of independence and courage
who sang the peasant songs of her region.
Later she recited the names of small mountain
villages like a litany that would protect
us against the rise of darkness and the fall
of hundreds of desperate men no longer
willing to pull in the fields or the factories
of Torino for a few lire and a Thank You.
She told me of those men, my uncles
and cousins, with names like water pouring
from stone jugs. Primo Grunwald,
Carlo Finzi, Mario Antonio Todesco, Beniamino
Levi, my grandfather. They would die,
she said, as my father had died, because all
of these lands of ours were angered. No one
remembered the simple beauty of a clear dawn
and how snow fell covering the streets
littered with lies. Toward dawn she rose
and watched the light graying the still waters
and held me to the window and bobbed me up

and down until I awakened a moment to
see the golden sun splashed upon the eye
of the world. You wonder why I am
impossible, why I stand in the bus station
in Toledo baying No! No! and hurling
the luggage of strangers every which way,
why I refuse to climb ladders or descend into
cellars of coal dust and dead mice or eat
like a good boy or change my dirty clothes
no matter who complains. Look in my eyes!
They have stared into the burning eyes of earth,
molten metals, the first sun, a woman's face,
they have seen the snow covering it all
and a new day breaking over the mother sea.
I breathed the truth. I was born in Lucerne.

SALT

This one woman has been sobbing
for hours. The last plane has gone,
and no one is left except the porter
mopping the floors and an old woman
cleaning out the ash trays and wiping
the chrome handles of the chairs.
No one has asked her to leave because
there are no mores flights and even the cop
down the tiled hall has fallen asleep.
The plane has by now entered the night
somewhere between Chicago and Cleveland,
and below the lights of cities are going
on and off or perhaps there are cloud banks
or perhaps the man in the window seat
is blinking his eyes. Soon they will
pass over water. No one will think,
Thus did the Angel of Death before he
descended upon Egypt only to find
the Egyptians, though many will think
of death as the darkness below. One
or two may pray to enter it, tonight,
while there is still time to die all
at once in a great jellied ball of fire,
brief stars torn from their orbits. Landing,
the passengers scatter in all directions
and disappear into the city in cabs, on buses,
in subway cars. Some find someone waiting
and walk whispering arm in arm toward the car.
One man stands in the faint drizzle
and puts on his rain coat and hat. If he
hurries he can be home by dinner, and he
and his kids can watch television until
one by one they fall asleep before the set
and dream of those dark stretches that redeem
nothing at all or of the rain that hangs
above the city swollen with red particles
of burned air. One of them, perhaps the father,

may even dream of tears which must always fall
because water and salt were given us
at birth to make what we could of them,
and being what we are we chose love
and having found it we lost it over and over.

ASCENSION

Now I see the stars
are ready for me
and the light falls upon
my shoulders evenly,
so little light that even
the night birds can't see
me robed in black flame.
I am alone, rising
through clouds and the lights
of distant cities until
the earth turns its darker
side away, and I am ready
to meet my guardians
or speak again the first words
born in time. Instead
it is like that dream
in which a friend leaves
and you wait, parked
by the side of the road
that leads home until
you can feel your skin
wrinkling and your hair
grown long and tangling
in the winds and still you
wait because you've waited
so long. Below, the earth
has turned to light but
unlike the storied good
in Paradise I see no going
and coming, none of the pain
I would have suffered had I
merely lived. At first
I can remember my wife,
the immense depth of her eyes
and her smooth brow in morning
light, the long lithe body
moving about her garden

day after day, at ease in the light
of those brutal summers. I can
see my youngest son again
moving with the slight swagger
of the carpenter hitching
up his belt of tools. I
can even remember the feel
of certain old shirts
against my back and shoulders
and how my arms ached
after a day of work. Then I
forget exhaustion, I forget
love, forget the need to
be a man, the need to
speak the truth, to close
my eyes and talk to someone
distant but surely listening.
Then I forget my own trees
at evening moving in the day's
last heat like the children
of the wind, I forget the hunger
for food, for belief, for love,
I forget the fear of death,
the fear of living forever,
I forget my brother, my name,
my own life. I have risen.
Somewhere I am a God.
Somewhere I am a holy
object. Somewhere I am.

ROOFS

As a child I climbed the roof
and sat alone looking down
at my own back yard, no longer
the same familiar garden.
I thought of flying, of spreading
my arms and pushing off,
but when I did I was back
to earth in no time, but now
with a broken hand that broke
the fall. From this I learned
nothing so profound as Newton
might, but something about
how little truth there was
in fantasy. I had seen that
gesture into air on Saturdays
in the Avalon Theater, where
unfailingly men and women soared
and alighted delicately and with
a calm that suggested they'd
done nothing. My hand bandaged,
I climbed back up and sat
staring over the orderly roofs
to where a steeple rose
or a fire house tolled its bell.
I'd learned something essential
about all that was to come.
The clouds passing over, as I
lay back, were only clouds,
not faces, animals, or portents.
They might carry a real water
that beat fire or knives
and surrendered only to stones,
but no more. The way down
was just like the way up, one
foot following another until
both were firmly on the ground.
Now even a twelve year old

could see he hadn't gone far,
though it was strangely silent
there at the level of high branches,
nothing in sight but blue sky
a little closer and more familiar,
always calling me back as though
I'd found by accident or as in
a dream my only proper element.

I WANTED YOU TO KNOW

Little yellow tufts of grass grew
even in our front yard. 1937.
The chow down the block snarled
when I passed. He had a black nose
and would strain, choking himself,
against his leash. I tried going
the long way around the block, but
those kids called me terrible names,
and my brother and I fought them until
we were all crying. Behind the station
was an abandoned convertible I drove
from there to Chicago chased by dogs.
When Davey and his mom moved in
downstairs, the lady next door said
the neighborhood was going. Her son,
Clark, called Davey "Abie" and threw
a potato through the kitchen window.
Later the police came and took him
for stealing a car. We made guns
that shot strips of rubber cut
from tire tubes and played at war
in the alleys and garages until
the first snows came. The late sun
was golden along my arm, the heat
was pleasant, not at all like burning,
and I sat alone in the living room
while the radio spoke of men freezing
in the mountains of Spain. They died,
and some of the men up there were ours,
and their names were secret. When bombs
fell on Shanghai I got a picture card
with my bubble gum that showed blades
of window glass killing grown people
and children and a great hotel turned
to red and yellow flames. At night I
slept alone, deep in my bed, the covers
over my head and dreamed of coins

that made a trail to a box of gold.
I never dreamed of war planes diving
on undefended cities, of the Czechs
abandoned and lost, of German soldiers
entering the Ruhr, of my own brother
leaving on a train for basic training.
In the spring that followed I planted
my first tomato, and I hauled loads
of rocks in my wagon to help my mother
build her special kind of garden.
At the drug store I bought, wrapped
in burlap, a tiny rose bush, just
a stick, for her birthday, April 12th.
The next year there were four buds
that were red, not yellow, as she'd
wanted, not the tea roses, as she
called them, that were her favorites.
Before the month had passed, they became
four tight little blooms, eyes closed,
just touched with rain. They were mine,
and the whole world was never the same.

NEVER BEFORE

Never before
have I gone down
on my hands and knees
and begged the earth to stop turning
in its burning sleep
Never before have I asked the sky
why the rain no longer smears
the eyes of this blind house
why the day never again wakens
with the old washed clarity
in which the green new oranges
bob in their rough skins
toward winter and the coming year
Never before
have I turned my whole road
homeward to this one heart
and asked why I am cinders
why I stand in the dawn winds
and cannot smell the coming of day
why I see the white lip of the Pacific
curling back from land and want
to fall through centuries of unchartered water
toward the frozen center
Will the grass answer
if I bow to it
it is late in the year
and it blows in the autumn chill
blond and careless
the flag of no one
turning slowly to straw or weed
burning in the wasted lot of my life
Never before
have I gone back to the place where I began
and found miles of scattered buildings
rags that were clothes, broken bottles
dishes, yards of burned tires
hills of broken fans, tired motors

dogs, the rubble of lives
that were not lives
and found my own home gone, so much space
filled with the yellow air
we must not breathe
Never before
have I seen in the dark eyes
of children a flame growing slowly
that will scorch first their own hair
and then turn my eyes to fire
never before have I been afraid
as they stood close and not touching
watching me turn back
toward my car and drive away
until the winds whispered *stop*
and I could sit for a moment
remembering what it was
to rise slowly to a world
that seemed at peace on the long
Sunday mornings of lonely first manhood
when I knew nothing
except there was no work that day
When I ask that man
why he wakened in the dark
and dressed himself in the same dirty clothes
that lay on the floor
and drank only cold water
he answers *Monday*
as though that meant
a basket of fresh laundry before his door
or the soil wakening in long rows
to the tiny fists of new shoots
and not the slam of iron on iron
the hands chewing themselves
to rags of blood and loose skin
Never before
have I heard my own voice

cry out in a language not mine
that the earth was wrong
that night came first and then nothing
that birds flew only to their deaths
that ice was the meaning of change
that I was never a child
nor were you nor were my lost sons
nor the sons they won't have
Never before
has dawn streaked the sky
with the purple wastes of iron
has noon turned in the shadows
of small circles of fallen gray leaves
has evening seen the cows
refuse to return
to their long glowing sheds
they shake, they drop their heads
because they must
the hillsides are rusting
the rocks tumble down
so many dull lumps that shatter
into clods of slag
climb higher while the light
still holds out
there is the valley where we came
to rest after turning through water
through generations of earth, through fire
there is the last dust
rising toward the sun
Never before
have our whole lives
danced in the slow light
of the last hour
never before have I taken
your hand and found
five soiled pages
never before have I taken my own

and found something I had not seen
blood that was heavy and slow
tarnished skin smelling like old breath
bones that laughed
my right arm is
a river that runs toward the heart
bearing no wish
no hope no memory
a river without a name
that began nowhere
and soon will turn back
upon itself
my eyes are deserts
where nothing is
except the dust clouds gathering
far off in another place
until the sun pales
and they are overhead
and must burst
Never before
has the night come down
around me with the blinking
of an eye and the darkness
spread from me to hide it all
the hills behind me
and the scattered used-up farms below
the stale fields, the one horse
broken and old
already hidden in shadow
the old men womenless since birth
walking the roads
their hands folded behind them
their heads down and hatless
their voices at the old familiar prayers
that they will come back
never or to something else
Never before

have they stumbled on and on
in a language
I have forgotten
bowing and rising over
and over, so many stunted
roadside trees burning
as they hold on
and bearing nothing

THAT DAY

I woke in a cold room
near the port. I rose and dressed
and went downstairs for coffee,
but the cooks were arguing
over *futbol* and didn't see me.
So I walked the shadowed streets
until I came to the old burned
cathedral of Santa Maria del Mar.
Inside I knew there were women
in black praying for those
they'd turned away from in life
and the smell of candles so old
you could almost hear them
hissing against the voices. Now
and then the wind moved up high
in the ancient lofts, and so I entered
to hear the odd music we and
the world have made of death.
I sat in the back and bowed my head
and closed my eyes. The voices came
to me, first the voice of a child
afraid to become a woman. I hoped
she was promised to become whatever
she chose to be. She stood and left
carrying her school books. Someone
thanked all the saints for the loss
of her pain in elbow, knee, and foot,
someone asked for peace and her son's
return from the streets of war,
someone rang out in anger against
a lifetime at sea. And high above
the wind sang through the stones
as though it recalled that once men
prayed here and waited until the air
told them to go. An hour passed,
and the place grew still as though
each prayer were answered, each cry

taken to a heart that cares. Outside
the sun was blinding on the stones,
sand-blasted or new, and the city
had risen to face another Monday
shrill with the smells of garbage
and gasoline. The sea was there, graying,
as it had for years, and the faces of men
and women turned downward to see
the world that once loved us, the world
we will eat cinder by cinder until
we can hold no more. I could ask
the sea to forget, the sky to rename
itself and become a banner of hope,
I could ask the children to grow
into life and their God to rise from stone,
but this was an ordinary day of millions
of days in the cities of the world,
and so all I can do is tell you this.

YOU CAN CRY

I am in an empty house, and the wind
is blowing the eucalyptus so that the branches
sway slowly with a great sea sound,
and although it is dark, I know their movement
having seen it at dusk for years of summer
when the long day's last winds rose suddenly.
The five great branches lifted in soft light
and let their dusty leaves hold the moment
and then settled back with the long sigh
of an old man at that hour setting
down his tools. And I remember that man,
Old Cherry, his black head running with gray,
bowed in his bib overalls, letting the scarred
handle of the sledge hammer slide through
his thick fingers and burying his ashen face
in a red bandana, twenty-eight years ago
beside a road long since dismantled
and hauled off in truck-loads of broken bits.
If he rose now from the earth of Michigan
where he rests in the streaming gowns
of his loss, Old Cherry Dorn, and walked
over the whole dark earth with one hand
stretched out to touch a single thing
he'd made in a lifetime, he would cross
this continent to where the last sea fills
the night and his one sigh is lost in sea sounds.
That is the sea, that is the moment that fills
my house with the wailing of all we've lost
until there is nothing left but dust falling
into dust, either in darkness or in the first
long rays of yellow light that are waiting
behind the eastern ranges. Do you hear
the moaning of those great lifting arms? That
is the sea of all our unshed tears, that is all
anyone can finally hear, so you can cry,
Cherry, you can cry forever and no one will know.

THE CONDUCTOR OF NOTHING

If you were to stop and ask me
how long I have been as I am,
a man who hates nothing
and rides old trains for the sake
of riding, I could only answer
with that soft moan I've come
to love. It seems a lifetime I've
been silently crossing and recrossing
this huge land of broken rivers
and fouled lakes, and no one has cared
enough even to ask for a ticket
or question this dingy parody
of a uniform. In the stale,
echoing stations I hunch over a paper
or ply the air with my punch
and soon we are away, pulling out
of that part of a city where the backs
of shops and houses spill out
into the sunlight and the kids
sulk on the stoops or run aimlessly
beneath the viaducts. Then we are
loose, running between grassy slopes
and leaving behind the wounded
wooden rolling stock of another era.
Ahead may be Baltimore, Washington,
darkness, the string of empty cars
rattling and jolting over bad track,
and still farther up ahead the dawn
asleep now in some wet wood far
south of anywhere you've ever been,
where it will waken among the ghostly
shapes of oak and poplar, the ground fog
rising from the small abandoned farms
that once could feed a people. Thus
I come back to life each day
miraculously among the dead,
a sort of moving monument

to what a man can never be—
someone who can say "yes" or "no"
kindly and with a real meaning,
and bending to hear you out, place
a hand upon your shoulder, open
my eyes fully to your eyes, lift
your burden down, and point the way.

RAIN

Rain falling on the low-built houses
that climb the back of this mountain,
rain streaming down the pocked roads
and bringing with it the hard yellow earth
in little rivers that blacken my shoes,
speechless as ever, like shy animals.
I wait in the doorway of a tobacco shop
and the men go in and out cursing the season.
They light up before they step back into it,
shoulders hunched, heads down, starting
up the long climb to a house of wet cardboard
and makeshift paper windows. No, this
is not the island of Martinique or Manhattan
or the capitol of sweet airs or the dome
of heaven or hell, many colored, splendid.
This is an ordinary gray Friday after work
and before dark in a city of the known world.

KEEP TALKING

If it ain't simply this, what is it?
he wanted to know, and she answered,
"If it ain't this it ain't nothing,"
and they turned off the light, locked
the door, and went downstairs and out
of the hotel and started looking around
for a bar that would stay open all night.
In the first one she said, "When do
you close?" The bartender said, "What's
yours?" Then he got mad, her man,
because she'd asked politely, and so
he shouted, "Please answer the question."
Then he said, "How late are you open?"
"Until the law says we gotta close."
They went out into the early summer
which was still light even though
kids were probably already in bed.
The wind stood out against the sails
on the sound, and the last small boats
were coming in on the blackening waters.
After a while he said, "Maybe we could
just eat and take a long walk or sit
somewhere for a while and say things."
She didn't answer. The wind had picked
up and just might have blown his words
into nothing. "Why don't we talk?"
he said. She turned and stared right
into his eyes, which were light blue
and seemed to be bulging out with tears.
He was unshaven and wore a wool cap
which he'd removed. "I've been here
before," he said, "as a boy I wanted
to talk about things, but there was no
one to talk to." "Talk to me," she said.
"I don't know what to say. I didn't
know then." "When?" she said. "When
I was a boy." So she explained that

being a kid was not knowing what to say
but that now he was a grown man. The lights
of the city were coming on, the high
ones in the tall buildings repeated
themselves in the still waters now as dark
as the night would ever be. He thought
about what she'd said and was sure
it had been different, that other kids
spoke about who they were or walked
with each other and said all the things
that jumbled in his head then and now.
He sat down on the curb and pressed
his face into his knees. She just stood
looking down at the shaven white back
of his neck, thin and childish, and she
thought, If it ain't this what is it?

ABOVE JAZZ

> "A friend tells me he has risen above
> jazz. I leave him there . . ." Michael Harper

There is that music that the hammer
makes when it hits the nail squarely
and the wood opens with a sigh. There is
the music of the bones growing, of
teeth biting into bread, of the baker
making bread, slapping the dusted loaf
as though it were a breathing stone.
There has always been the music
of the stars, soundless and glittering
in the winter air, and the moon's
full song, loon-like and heard only
by someone far from home who glances
up to the southern sky for help and finds
the unfamiliar cross and for a moment
wonders if he or the heavens
have lost their way. Most perfect
is the music heard in sleep—the breath
suspends itself above the body, the soul
returns to the room having gone in dreams
to some far shore and entered water
only to rise and fall again and rise
a final time dressed in the rags of time
and made the long trip home to the body,
cast-off and senseless, because it is
the only instrument it has. Listen, stop
talking, stop breathing. That is music,
whatever you hear, even if it's
only the simple pulse, the tides
of blood tugging toward the heart
and back on the long voyage that must
always take them home. Even if you
hear nothing, the breathless earth
asleep, the oceans at last at rest,
the sun frozen before dawn and the peaks
of the eastern mountains upright, cold,

and silent. All that you do not hear
and never can is music, and in the dark
creation dances around the single center
that would be listening if it could.

THE WINDOW

To you it is a colorless eye
on the sleeping world. The faint light
it brings illuminates the fields
behind our old farmhouse, trees,
barns, low hills, an absence
of animal life in the hushed house
of your human head. There
is a bald path that winds
darkly among dilapidated sheds
and the ruins of small winter gardens,
and in your mind you follow
along the overgrown banks
to a small pond, the surface
just stilled after the noisy rising
heavenward of some great white bird,
an egret possibly or a swan
who this time is only a swan.
You gaze up, aware that the wind
scatters your long hair going
gradually gray and tangling, aware too
that the one tear that slides
from the burning corner of an eye
is freighted with neither joy
or sorrow but glistens on
your glowing cheek like a globe
of liquid fire and contains all
the hundred and more colors
of the spectrum and is a perfect
lens through which the world
returns to water and once more
we bear the sighs of the drowned
and the silence of the still-to-be.
Now daylight pours in this window,
and you see the shadows of doors,
chest, bed, desk, and you wonder
what tiny animals are frozen
in that dark, their eyes enormous

with fear or wonder, and you close
your own eyes and count to ten
ten times so that all those caught
by the dawn far from nest or burrow
can return. By this time
I've awakened, yawned, risen
and put on my pants, stumbling first
on the left foot, then on the right,
padded barefoot across the room
and down the stairs to see
if anyone has brought the milk,
the morning newspaper, or stolen
the hubcaps from my Pontiac.

HAVING BEEN ASKED
"WHAT IS A MAN?" I ANSWER
after Keats

My oldest son comes to visit me
in the hospital. He brings giant
peonies and the nurse puts them
in a glass vase, and they sag quietly
on the windowsill where they
seem afraid to gaze out at the city
smoking beneath. He asks when I
will be coming home. I don't know.
He sees there are wires running
from me to a television set on which
my heartbeat is the Sunday Spectacular.
How do I look? I say. He studies
the screen and says, I don't know.
It takes a specialist to tell you how
you look in this place, and none will.
I must have slept, and when I waken
I am alone, and the old man
next to me is gone, and the room
is going dark. This is the Sunday
that will fill the unspoken promise
of all those vanished Sundays
when a shadow on the edge of sight
grew near, enormous, hesitated, and left,
and I sighed with weariness knowing
one more week was here to live.
At last a time and place to die are
given me, and even a small reason.
The flowers have turned now that
the windows have gone dark, and I
see their pale faces in the soft mirror
of the glass. No, they aren't crying,
for this is not the vale of tears.
They are quietly laughing as flowers
always do in the company of men.
"Because this is the place where souls

are made," their laughter whispers.
I will read Keats again, I will rise
and go into the world, unwired and free,
because I am no longer a movie,
I have no beginning, no middle, no end,
no film score underscoring each act,
no costume department, no expert on color.
I am merely a man dressing in the dark
because that is what a man is—
so many mouthfuls of laughter
and so many more, all there can be
behind the sad brown backs of peonies.

II

ONE FOR THE ROSE

Three weeks ago I went back
to the same street corner where
27 years before I took a bus for Akron,
Ohio, but now there was only a blank space
with a few concrete building blocks
scattered among the beer cans
and broken bottles and a view of
the blank backside of an abandoned hotel.
I wondered if Akron was still down there
hidden hundreds of miles south among
the small, shoddy trees of Ohio,
a town so ripe with the smell
of defeat that its citizens lied
about their age, their height, sex,
income, and previous condition
of anything. I spent all of a Saturday
there, disguised in a cashmere suit
stolen from a man twenty pounds
heavier than I, and I never unbuttoned
the jacket. I remember someone
married someone, but only the bride's
father and mother went out
on the linoleum dance floor and leaned
into each other like whipped school kids.
I drank whatever I could find and made
my solitary way back to the terminal
and dozed among the drunks and widows
toward dawn and the first thing north.
What was I doing in Akron, Ohio
waiting for a bus that groaned slowly
between the sickened farms of 1951
and finally entered the smeared air
of hell on US 24 where the Rouge plant
destroys the horizon? I could have been
in Paris at the foot of Gertrude Stein,
I could have been drifting among
the reeds of a clear stream

like the little Moses, to be found
by a princess and named after a conglomerate
or a Jewish hero. Instead I was born
in the wrong year and in the wrong place,
and I made my way so slowly and badly
that I remember every single turn,
and each one smells like an overblown rose,
yellow, American, beautiful, and true.

THE FOX

I think I must have lived
once before, not as a man or woman
but as a small, quick fox pursued
through fields of grass and grain
by ladies and gentlemen on horseback.
This would explain my nose
and the small dark tufts of hair
that rise from the base of my spine.
It would explain why I am
so seldom invited out to dinner
and when I am I am never
invited back. It would explain
my loathing for those on horseback
in Central Park and how I can
so easily curse them and challenge
the men to fight and why no matter
how big they are or how young
they refuse to dismount,
for at such times, rock in hand,
I must seem demented.
My anger is sudden and total,
for I am a man to whom anger
usually comes slowly, spreading
like a fever along my shoulders
and back and turning my stomach
to a stone, but this fox anger
is lyrical and complete, as I stand
in the pathway shouting and refusing
to budge, feeling the dignity
of the small creature menaced
by the many and larger. Yes,
I must have been that unseen fox
whose breath sears the thick bushes
and whose eyes burn like opals
in the darkness, who humps
and shits gleefully in the horsepath
softened by moonlight and goes on

45

feeling the steady measured beat
of his fox heart like a wordless
delicate song, and the quick forepaws
choosing the way unerringly
and the thick furred body following
while the tail flows upward,
too beautiful a plume for anyone
except a creature who must proclaim
not ever ever ever
to mounted ladies and their gentlemen.

MAKING SODA POP

The big driver said
he only fucked Jews. Eddie smiled
and folded his glasses
into their little blue
snap case and put the case
into his lunch bag. Last night
I think she was your sister.
This was noon
on the loading docks
at Mavis-Nu-Icy-Bottling,
Eddie and I side by side
our backs to the wall,
our legs stretched out
before us the way children
do on a sofa. Ain't got
no sister, Eddie said.
Must have been
your mother then. Eddie
landed first
and the man, older and slower,
fell back out of the shade
into the cinders
of the rail yard. The guy
beside me went on chewing.
Eddie came slowly forward
crouching, his weak eyes
wide, and swung
again, again, and the man
went down heavier
this time and didn't
try to get up. Eddie
came back to his place
beside me, no smile on
his face, nothing, and opened
a peanut butter sandwich.
Alvin, the foreman, looked up
and said, OK, you guys,
this afternoon cream soda.

EACH DAWN

Each dawn I die
and waken at dusk
to swim into the darkness
coming in from the far fields.
The orchards of plum
and almonds, the hillsides
spotted with gnarled olives,
under which the long shadows
of afternoon slept, I seemed
to be waiting there
to fill your wide eyes.
You are the same, young
and trusting, moving at ease
from the small plot
of herbs and sunflowers
where you weeded and sang
all afternoon. You swing
your shoulders as you descend
the hill toward the old white
stuccoed farm house, wailing
your pleasure in being you,
singing to the foolish quail,
grown fat and trusting, and to
what is left of a day
you grew to love. I am
what is left. Do you feel
me suddenly sliding lightly
across those frail shoulders
oiled with sweat? Do you
see me rising in the little
cyclones of dust twisting
across the fallow fields?
It doesn't matter. I have
entered you everywhere
so quietly your smile remains
the same. Your eyes seem
frozen with joy, your voice

high and soft. Only your blood
sliding toward the heart
has darkened and slowed,
but before the light fails
I will arrive, I will.

THE RADIO

Another morning, I rose before work
and played the radio, dance music
from Canada, and I imagined men
and women far older than I gathered
at some seaside hotel and dancing
cheek to cheek in the style the films
made romantic. Dressed in formals,
the women were flushed pink, and beads
of perspiration stood out across
their foreheads. The men were
working men, dressed up in dark
heavy wool suits even in summer,
and they swung their thickened bodies
like small boats in rough waters.
I had not yet gone to dances, and I
envied them, I envied them these women,
plain as they were and saying, "Gosh,
it's awful hot here!" I envied
their lives, fixed as they were toward
some round of forty years of work
and then nothing I could then imagine.
Was it my father who years before
had spoken of such scenes? Books
I'd read? Movies? I remember a word
that fell from the radio when I
was no more than seven. A man
said his "destiny" was still before
him and uncertain, and I saw miles
of great sand dunes rising and falling
as on some Sahara and that man
searching day after day for what
I couldn't know and finally going hungry,
blind, crazy from the heat maybe,
and never heard from again. I sat
smoking my final cigarette before I
dressed and left for work and wondering
was it there ahead today for me,

what men and women searched for
all their lives. And would I know
it when at last it fell into my life
as I knew those trite and simple tunes
I heard every morning and danced to,
womanless, twenty-four, and unafraid?

DEPOT BAY

100 miles south of Sydney
I watched the sea curve in
to the black volcanic reef
I stood upon, and imagined
the great meadows of the sea
that stretched between me
and anyone who knew my name
or cared for me. I would walk
back to the borrowed cabin, fall
on a cot, and dream of flight
over water, a singular bird
rising and falling in the winds,
and I would waken near dark
sweating lightly in my clothes
and not knowing for one moment
where I was. Then I would rise
and shave and take a last walk
under a spray of stars that meant
nothing to me. Thus I passed
five lonely days at Depot Bay,
and someone came in a Land Rover
to take me back to Canberra,
and I flew to Sydney. I spoke
to bus drivers and mailmen,
got directions from anyone,
met people like those I'd left
at home and forgot the still sea
and the bird fluttering like light.
The woman I took to dinner
died of cancer one year later,
the man whose hand rested
on my neck when he searched
my eyes forgot my name and now
writes me as David, that winter
which was summer here lost
whatever it was that made it
unlike any other. All of me

that was there has passed
into what I remember: the sea
rocking the deep cradle of all
of us and water and salt without
end in which we turned this way
and that, holding an unknown face
that rose out of nothing
and sank back, and one bird
going out on a column of light
and nothing ever returning
except the wind, wordless
and wild, filling everything.

GENIUS

Two old dancing shoes my grandfather
gave the Christian Ladies,
an unpaid water bill, the rear license
of a dog that messed on your lawn,
a tooth I saved for the good fairy
and which is stained with base metals
and plastic filler. With these images
and your black luck and my bad breath
a bright beginner could make a poem
in fourteen rhyming lines about the purity
of first love or the rose's many thorns
or the dew that won't wait long enough
to stand my little gray wren a drink.

ONE

When I was only a child I carried
a little wooden sword in my belt
and with it I could face the dark,
I could descend the shaky steps
to the basement and there enter
each shadowed corner and even stare
at the thousand tearful eyes
of the coal bin. Later, still
a boy, I heard my brother crying
in his bed next to mine, not
for fear of the dark or because
the dead would not return or
for the dull ache of his growing.
In December of '51 on the night shift
a plain woman from West Virginia
began suddenly to curse this life.
She untied the rag that hid
her graying hair and wiped her face
and still the words came. "It's shit.
That's just what it is, shit." No one
answered or took her in his arms
or held her hand, and before long
she'd bowed her head to the wheel
that polished the new chromed tubes,
and all our hours passed a moment
at a time and disappeared somewhere
in the vast unchartered spaces between
the moons of our blood. Now if I
stood before myself naked in my body
flecked with graying hairs, I would cry
out that I too am still only a boy
and the great vein that climbs down
my shoulder and into my right hand
stumbles under the will of heaven.
I am burning in this new summer,
I am one with the scattered roses,
one with the moon waning long

before dawn, one with my brother
who has come down from the sky
and that long lost woman who told
the truth and received at daybreak
one toothless kiss on her forehead
from our father and mother the rain.

THE DOCTOR OF STARLIGHT

"Show me the place," he said.
I removed my shirt and pointed
to a tiny star above my heart.
He leaned and listened. I could feel
his breath falling lightly, flattening
the hairs on my chest. He turned
me around, and his hands gently
plied my shoulder blades and then rose
to knead the twin columns forming
my neck. "You are an athlete?"
"No," I said, "I'm a working man."
"And you make?" he said. "I make
the glare for lightbulbs." "Yes,
where would we be without them?"
"In the dark." I heard the starched
dress of the nurse behind me,
and then together they helped me
lie face up on his table, where blind
and helpless I thought of all
the men and women who had surrendered
and how little good it had done them.
The nurse took my right wrist
in both of her strong hands, and I
saw the doctor lean toward me,
a tiny chrome knife glinting in
one hand and tweezers in the other.
I could feel nothing, and then he said
proudly, "I have it!" and held up
the perfect little blue star, no
longer me and now bloodless. "And do
you know what we have under it?"
"No," I said. "Another perfect star."
I closed my eyes, but the lights
still swam before me in a sea
of golden fire. "What does it mean?"
"Mean?" he said, dabbing the place
with something cool and liquid,

and all the lights were blinking on
and off, or perhaps my eyes were
opening and closing. "Mean?" he said,
"It could mean this is who you are."

THE FIRST TRUTH

The second truth is that the rose blooms
and the dark petals burn to dust or wind,
and when nothing is left someone remembers
it was once spring and hurries through the snow
on the way home from a day's work, his
quilted jacket bunched high about his neck
against the steady December wind. The day
ends before anyone is ready, even
this single man who lives alone and feeds
two stray cats and himself on large tins
of exotic ocean fish drowned in mustard sauce
or unpeeled potatoes boiled and left to cool.
He sings as he shaves, staring into his eyes
which to him are as mysterious as the eyes
of the two striped cats or the dark eyes
of the black woman who worked beside him
all that day and sighed just the once, after
she'd finished her small lunch of soda pop
and processed cheese and stood up to return
to her job. She wore a small wedding ring
and a gold cross on a gold chain. In the mirror
he sees his own silver chain disappear under
his shirt and the thick arms that want to crush
someone he has never known against his body
and stand in silence, warm against the wind,
which he knows is blowing because it blew
that morning on the way to work and that evening
on the way back. He stands, half-shaven, staring
into a face that is suddenly his own face
which has given him a name ever since he could speak.
He steps back as far as he can to see all of the man
he would give up if you knocked at his door.

TO CIPRIANO, IN THE WIND

Where did your words go,
Cipriano, spoken to me 38 years
ago in the back of Peerless Cleaners,
where raised on a little wooden platform
you bowed to the hissing press
and under the glaring bulb the scars
across your shoulders—"a gift
of my country"—gleamed like old wood.
"*Dignidad*," you said into my boy's
wide eyes, "without is no riches."
And Ferrente, the dapper Sicilian
coatmaker, laughed. What could
a pants presser know of dignity?
That was the winter of '41, it
would take my brother off to war,
where you had come from, it would
bring great snowfalls, graying
in the streets, and the news of death
racing through the halls of my school.
I was growing. Soon I would be
your height, and you'd tell me
eye to eye, "Some day the world
is ours, some day you will see."
And your eyes burned in your fine
white face until I thought you
would burn. That was the winter
of '41, Bataan would fall
to the Japanese and Sam Baghosian
would make the long march
with bayonet wounds in both legs,
and somehow in spite of burning acids
splashed across his chest and the acids
of his own anger rising toward his heart
he would return to us and eat
the stale bread of victory. Cipriano,
do you remember what followed
the worst snow? It rained all night

and in the dawn the streets gleamed,
and within a week wild phlox leaped
in the open fields. I told you
our word for it, "Spring," and you said,
"Spring, spring, it always come after."
Soon the Germans rolled east
into Russia and my cousins died. I
walked alone in the warm spring winds
of evening and said, "Dignity." I said
your words, Cipriano, into the winds.
I said, "Someday this will all be ours."
Come back, Cipriano Mera, step
out of the wind and dressed in the robe
of your pain tell me again that this
world will be ours. Enter my dreams
or my life, Cipriano, come back
out of the wind.

BELIEF

No one believes in the calm
of the North Wind after a time
of rage and depression.
No one believes the sea cares nothing
for the shore or that
the long black volcanic reefs
that rise and fall from sight
each day are the hands
of some forgotten creature
trying to touch the unknowable
heart of water. No one believes
that the lost breath of a man
who died in 1821 is my breath
and that I will live until
I no longer want to, and then
I will write my name
in water, as he did, and pass
this breath to anyone who can
believe that life comes back
again and again without end
and always with the same face—
the face that broke in daylight
before the waves at Depot Bay
curling shoreward over and over
just after dawn as the sky cracked
into long slender fingers of light
and I heard your breath beside me
calm and sweet as you returned
to the dark crowded harbor of sleep.
That man will never return. He ate
the earth and the creatures of the sea
and the air, and so it is time he fed
the small tough patches of grass
that fight for water and air
between the blocks on the long walk
to and from school, it is time
that whatever he said began

first to echo and then fade
in the mind of no one
who listened, and that the bed
that moaned under his weight
be released, and that his shoes curl
upward at last and die, for they too
were only the skins of other animals,
not the bear or tiger he prayed to be
before he knew he too was animal,
but the slow ox that sheds his flesh
so that we might grow to our full height—
the beasts no one yearns to become
as young men dream of the sudden fox
threading his way up the thick hillside
and the old of the full-bellied seal,
whiskered and wisely playful. At the beach
at Castelldefels in 1965 a stout man
in his bare socks stood
above two young women stretched out
and dressed in almost nothing.
In one hand he held his vest,
his shoes, and his suit jacket
and with the other he pointed to those
portions of them he most admired,
and he named them in the formal,
guttural Spanish of the Catalan gentleman.
He went away with specks of fine sand
caught on his socks to remind him
that to enter the fire is to be burned
and that the finger he pointed would
blacken in time and probe the still earth,
root-like, stubborn, and find its life
in darkness. No one believes he
knew all this and dared the sea
to rise that moment and take him
away on a journey without end
or that the bodies of the drowned collect

light from the farthest stars and rise
at night to glow without song.
No one believes that to die
is beautiful, that after the hard pain
of the last unsaid word I am swept
in a calm out from shore
and hang in the silence of millions
for the first time among all my family
and that the magic of water
which has filled me becomes me
and I flow into every crack and crevice
where light can enter. Even my oak
takes me to heart. I shadow the yard
where you come in the evening
to talk while the light rises slowly
skyward, and you shiver a moment
before you go in, not believing
my voice in your ear and that the tall trees
blowing in the wind are sea sounds.
No one believes that tonight is the journey
across dark water to the lost continent
no one named. Do you hear the wind
rising all around you? That comes
only after this certain joy. Do you hear
the waves breaking, even in the darkness,
radiant and full? Close your eyes, close
them and follow us toward the first light.

RAIN DOWNRIVER

It has been raining now since
long before dawn, and the windows
of the Arab coffee house of Delray
are steamed over and no one looks
in or out. If I were on my way
home from the great chemical plant
on a bus of sodden men, heads rolling
with each swerve or lurch, I would get
off just here by the pale pink temple
and walk slowly the one block back
and swing open the doors on blue smoke
and that blurred language in which two
plus two means the waters of earth
have no end or beginning. I would sit
down at an empty table and open
a newspaper in which the atoms
of each meaningless lie are weighed
and I would order one bitter cup
and formally salute the ceiling,
which is blue like heaven but is
coming down in long bandages
revealing the wounds of the last rain.
In this state, which is not madness
but Michigan, here in the suburbs
of the City of God, rain brings back
the gasoline we blew in the face
of creation and sulphur which will not
soften iron or even yellow rice.
If the Messenger entered now
and called out, You are my people!
the tired waiter would waken and bring
him a coffee and an old newspaper
so that he might read in the wrong words
why the earth gives each of us
a new morning to begin the day
and later brings darkness to hide
what we did with it. Rain in winter

65

began first in the mind of God
as only the smallest thought,
but as the years passed quietly
into each other leaving only
the charred remains of empty hands
and the one glass that never overflowed
it came closer like the cold breath
of someone who has run through snow
to bring you news of a first birth
or to give you his abrupt, wet blessing
on the forehead. So now I go back
out into it. From a sky I can
no longer see, the fall of evening
glistens around my shoulders that
also glisten, and the world is mine.

SOURCES

Fish scales, wet newspapers, unopened cans
of syrupy peaches, smoking tires,
houses that couldn't contain
even a single family without someone
going nuts, raping his own child
or shotgunning his wife. The oily floors
of filling stations where our cars
surrendered their lives and we called
it quits and went on foot to phone
an indifferent brother for help.
No, these are not the elements
of our lives, these are what we left
for our children to puzzle our selves
together so they might come to know
who they are.
                    But they won't wait.
This one has borrowed a pick-up and a bag
of nails and will spend the light of day
under the California sun singing the songs
the radio lets loose and pounding together
a prefabricated barn. This one lies
back at night before a television set,
a beer in one hand, and waits for
the phone to ring him awake, for
a voice out of the night to tell him
the meaning of the names that fell
together and by which he knows himself.
Out there in the harbor of New York
is Ellis Island, almost empty now
except for the wind that will never leave.
He thinks of the little girl, her name
pinned to her dress, all she is
held in a little bag.
                    My distant sons,
my unborn daughters, myself, we
can go on smiling in the face
of the freezing winds that tear down

the Hudson Valley and out to sea, winds
that turn our eyes to white tears, or under
the bland blue sky of this our Western
valley where you sweat until you
cannot hold your own hands. What do we have
today? A morning paper full of lies.
A voice out of nowhere that says, Keep
punching. Darkness that falls each night.
Sea winds that smell of fish scales.
Borrowed cars that won't start and if they did
would go nowhere. Names that mean Lover
of Horses, Hammer, First and Only, Last
but Not Least, Beloved of God. Each other.

THE SUIT

Dark brown pin-stripe, the trousers
rising almost to my armpits
and descending, pleated, to great
bellows at the knees, only to close
down just above my shoes. This
was my fine suit, made of God
knows what hard fiber that would
not give or crease. And such
shoulders as no one my height
and under 150 pounds has ever had,
and the great wide swooning lapel
of the double-breasted job buttoning
just below the crotch. So robed, I
was officially dubbed a punk or wild
motherfucker depending on the streets
I glided down. Three times I wore it
formally: first with red suspenders
to a high school dance where no one
danced except the chaperones, in a style
that minimized the fear of gonorrhea.
It was so dark no one recognized me,
and I went home, head down. Then to a party
to which almost no one came and those
who did counted the minutes until
the birthday cake with its armored
frosting was cut and we could flee.
And finally to the draft board where
I stuffed it in a basket with my shoes,
shirt, socks, and underclothes and was
herded naked with the others past doctors
half asleep and determined to find
nothing. That long day it cracked
from indifference or abuse, and so I wore it
on the night shift at Detroit Transmission
where day after day it grew darker and more
unrecognizably tattered like all my
other hopes for a singular life in a rich

world that would be of certain design:
just, proportioned, equal and different
for each of us and satisfying like that flush
of warmth that came with knowing
no one could be more ridiculous than I.

BUYING EARTH

Time was, when I was a boy
and a bird called down my name,
I went out to the open fields
at the edge of my town and opened
my eyes to the blazing sky
and heard in the turning earth
the great groan of the dead
as they came back to life.
I cried out the few words
I knew, my own name, and the name
of the earth, and so doing
I bought the earth forever.
It was summer. The trees greened.
The wild grasses grew to my waist,
and everywhere I turned I broke
open the hearts of seeds, and yet
there was no wounding, no crying
out against my being there
as I would later hear, for I
had not come into the shape
of a man. I loved the world
that loved me so, and I thought
then in the long twilight turning
for home that the more I lived
the more this love would grow,
and I would be a Prince of Earth
someday, tall and lean, moving
alone beneath my sky that let
the rainy winds bless my hair
or the tears of snow jewel brow
and hands. Before I was 16
those fields were gone, the trees
brought down with a cry that stopped
nothing. Pond, grove, roadless
meadows between town and town,
all gone. And I walked on
in a starless dark where nothing

spoke my name. And it was then
I became a man, heavy, broken
into earth and breaking the earth
so that all the ruined waters
and the milky froth of mills might
run back to the seas they'd fled.
Yes, I became a man that sold himself
hand by hand, hour by hour, name
by lost name until there was nothing
left to sell, nothing left to buy.

THE VOICE

Small blue flowers like points
of sky were planted to pin
the earth above me, and still
I went on reaching through leaf
and grass blade and the saw-toothed
arms of thistles for the sky
that dozed above my death.
When the first winter came
I slept and wakened in the late March
to hear the flooded fields
singing their hymns to the birds.
The birds returned. And so it was
that I began to learn what changes
I had undergone. Not as in
a sea change had I been pared
down to the white essential
bones, nor did I remain huddled
around the silence after the breath
stormed and collapsed. I was large,
at first a meadow where wild
mustard quivered in warm winds.
Then I slipped effortlessly up
the foothills overlooking
that great awakening valley.
Then it seemed I was neither
the valley below or the peaks above
but a great breathing silence
that turned slowly through darkness
and light, which were the same,
toward darkness and light. I
remember the first time I spoke
in a human voice. I had been
sweeping away the last of sunset
in a small rural town, and I
passed shuddering through a woman
on her solitary way home, her arms
loaded with groceries. She said,

Oh my God! as though she were
lost and frightened, and so I let
the light linger until she found
her door. In truth for a while
I was scared of myself, even
my name scared me, for that's
what I'd been taught, but in
a single round of seasons I saw
no harm could come from me, and now
I embrace whatever pleases me,
and the earth is my one home,
as it always was, the earth
and perhaps some day the sky too
and all the climbing things between.

STEEL

Foxtails, vines, black rocks, small streams,
thistles, and here and there a bright bird
leaping from branch to branch, and then
the whip bird uncoiling his wild song. We
climbed higher and higher through the dense
forest of eucalyptus until the sea broke
below and the bright golden shore curved
landward for a time and then jutted back
to hold the steel town of Woolongong
over which a brown scum rode. I thought,
This is just like home, and before me
flashed that distant Sunday afternoon
on which I waited at a railroad crossing
while the tanks, one to a car, their guns
dropped and frowning, passed for some
fifteen minutes, and I wondered how
many deaths they would contain and would
one be mine. It was my cousin, not I,
in Patton's army at a famous bridgehead.
His widow came to stay with us, still not
thirty, a silent woman, childless, asking
for nothing. Over thirty years ago,
and even here on a clear winter Sunday
at the other end of the world that life
intrudes asking still to be dealt with,
understood, accepted. Names I have lost,
faces with no more character than the moon,
swim up out of my life. Someone has found
a long vine, and we take turns swinging
out and back over a patch of rocks
and spikey bushes. I'm once again
a child on a children's outing. We will build
a small fire from fallen boughs and eat steak
and sausages and drink the soft dry wine,
and lie back in the late sun, dozing until
the first cold winds chill our brows.
At last, the ocean darkening against

a low sky breaks cold and persistent over
the pocked stones, and we watch in silence
at dusk a herd of deer descending through
the fringe of forest to drink cautiously
at an old well. I could name these people
I will never see again, the mother and child,
the young painter full of hopes, the one
returned from Italy, his face creased
and tight as he bowed before a tiny thorn bush
and said its name over and over. Now I can hear
over the sea roar the great rolling mills
of Woolongong and the breaking of metal
on metal in the tides of the mind. I see
men and women stand back to let it happen, as
though the sea could stop, or steel, or memory.

ON MY OWN

Yes, I only got here on my own.
Nothing miraculous. An old woman
opened her door expecting the milk,
and there I was, seven years old, with
a bulging suitcase of wet cardboard
and my hair plastered down and stiff
in the cold. She didn't say, "Come in,"
she didn't say anything. Her luck
had always been bad, so she stood
to one side and let me pass, trailing
the unmistakable aroma of badger
which she mistook for my underwear,
and so she looked upward, not
to heaven but to the cracked ceiling
her husband had promised to mend,
and she sighed for the first time
in my life that sigh which would tell
me what was for dinner. I found my room
and spread my things on the sagging bed:
the bright ties and candy-striped shirts,
the knife to cut bread, the stuffed weasel
to guard the window, the silver spoon
to turn my tea, the pack of cigarettes
for the life ahead, and at last
the little collection of worn-out books
from which I would choose my only name—
Morgan the Pirate, Jack Dempsey, the Prince
of Wales. I chose Abraham Plain
and went off to school wearing a cap
that said "Ford" in the right script.
The teachers were soft-spoken women
smelling like washed babies and the students
fierce as lost dogs, but they all hushed
in wonder when I named the 400 angels
of death, the planets sighted and unsighted,
the moment at which creation would turn
to burned feathers and blow every which way

in the winds of shock. I sat down
and the room grew quiet and warm. My eyes
asked me to close them. I did, and so
I discovered the beauty of sleep and that
to get ahead I need only say I was there,
and everything would open as the darkness
in my silent head opened onto seascapes
at the other end of the world, waves
breaking into mountains of froth, the sand
running back to become the salt savor
of the infinite. Mrs. Tarbox woke me
for lunch—a tiny container of milk
and chocolate cookies in the shape of Michigan.
Of course I went home at 3:30, with
the bells ringing behind me and four stars
in my notebook and drinking companions
on each arm. If you had been there
in your yellow harness and bright hat
directing traffic you would never
have noticed me—my clothes shabby
and my eyes bright—; to you I'd have been
just an ordinary kid. Sure, now you
know, now it's obvious, what with the light
of the Lord streaming through the nine
windows of my soul and the music of rain
following in my wake and the ordinary air
on fire every blessed day I waken the world.

I REMEMBER CLIFFORD

Wakening in a small room,
the walls high and blue, one high window
through which the morning enters,
I turn to the table beside me
painted a thick white. There instead
of a clock is a tumbler of water,
clear and cold, that wasn't there
last night. Someone quietly entered,
and now I see the white door
slightly ajar and around three sides
the light on fire. I remember once
twenty-seven yeas ago walking
the darkened streets
of my home town when up ahead
on Joy Road at the Bluebird of Happiness
I heard over the rumble of traffic
and the rumbling of my own head
for the first time the high clear trumpet
of Clifford Brown calling us all
to the dance he shared with us
such a short time. My heart quickened
and in my long coat, breathless
and stumbling, I ran
through the swirling snow
to the familiar sequined door
knowing it would open on something new.